I WONDER Why

Stars Twinkle

and other questions about space

Carole Stott

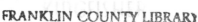

KINGFISHER
LONDON & NEW YORK

Copyright © 2011 by Kingfisher
Published in the United States by Kingfisher,
175 Fifth Ave., New York, NY 10010
Kingfisher is an imprint of Macmillan Children's Books,
London.
All rights reserved.

First published 1993 by Kingfisher
This edition published 2011 by Kingfisher

Distributed in the U.S. by Macmillan, 175 Fifth Ave.,
New York, NY 10010
Distributed in Canada by H.B. Fenn and Company Ltd.,
34 Nixon Road, Bolton, Ontario L7E 1W2

Library of Congress Cataloging-in-Publication data has
been applied for.

ISBN 978-0-7534-6551-6 (HC)
ISBN 978-0-7534-6520-2 (PB)

Kingfisher books are available for special promotions and
premiums. For details contact: Special Markets Department,
Macmillan, 175 Fifth Ave., New York, NY 10010.

For more information, please visit www.kingfisherbooks.com

Printed in China
9 8 7 6 5 4 3 2 1
1TR/1010/WKT/UNTD/140MA

Consultant: Dr. David Hughes, Sheffield University, U.K.
Illustrations: Chris Forsey cover, 4–5, 31; Ruby Green figure
artwork 19; Tony Kenyon (B.L. Kearley Ltd.) all cartoons;
Sebastian Quigley (Linden Artists) 6–15, 18–21, 28–29; Ian
Thompson 16–17, 22–25; Ross Watton (Garden Studio) 26–27

FOR OWEN

CONTENTS

What is the universe?

The whole world and everything beyond it is the universe. It is all the stars and planets, Earth and its plants and animals, you and me—everything.

You are made of the same stuff as a star!

There are huge groups of stars in space. They are called galaxies, and they're like gigantic star cities.

The big bang explosion sent the young universe flying out in all directions. Over very long periods of time, parts came together to make galaxies.

The galaxies are still speeding apart today, and the universe is getting bigger.

When did it all begin?

To see how the universe is getting bigger, watch the spots as you blow up a spotted balloon.

Many astronomers think that everything in the universe was once packed together in one small lump. Then, about 14 billion years ago, there was a gigantic explosion called the big bang.

Will the universe ever end?

Some astronomers think the universe will just continue getting bigger as the galaxies speed apart. Others think that the galaxies may one day start falling back toward one another until they crash together in a big crunch!

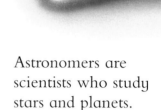

Astronomers are scientists who study stars and planets.

No one knows where all the material to make the universe came from in the first place.

What is the Milky Way?

The Milky Way is the galaxy we live in. It is made up of all the stars you can see in the sky at night, and many, many more you cannot see.

The Milky Way is a barred spiral galaxy. Below you can see what it looks like from above—a little like a whirlpool with long, spiraling arms.

Astronomers usually give galaxies numbers instead of names. Only a few have names that tell us what they look like—the Whirlpool, the Sombrero, and the Black Eye, for example.

The Milky Way got its name because at night we can sometimes see part of it as a band of milky white light across the sky.

From the side, a spiral galaxy looks like two fried eggs stuck together.

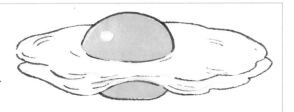

There are four main galaxy shapes. The barred spiral is one. Here are the others:

Irregular (no special shape)

Elliptical (egg-shaped)

We live on a planet called Earth, which travels around a star called the Sun.

Spiral

How many stars are there?

There are about one trillion stars in the Milky Way. That is almost 200 stars for every person living on Earth today!

Although we cannot see all of it, astronomers have figured out how big the universe is and how many stars it has. There are about 100 billion billion stars, in around 100 billion galaxies. It is hard to even think about so many stars, let alone count them all!

What are stars made of?

Sometimes, huge flamelike sheets of glowing gas shoot out from a star. These are called prominences.

Stars are not solid like the ground beneath your feet. Instead, they are made of gases like the air around you.

The two main gases in stars are hydrogen and helium. They are the stars' fuel. Stars make heat and light from them.

Since ancient times, stargazers have seen patterns in the way stars are grouped in the sky. These patterns are called constellations.

The brightest star we can see in the night sky is called Sirius. Another name for it is the Dog Star. It is about twice as big as our Sun, but it gives out more than 20 times as much light!

Why do stars twinkle?

Stars twinkle only when we look at them from Earth. Out in space, their light shines steadily. We see them twinkling and shimmering because of the air around Earth—as light from a star travels toward us, it is bent and wobbled by bubbles of hot and cold air.

Light bends when it passes through different things. If you put a straw in a glass of water, for example, it looks bent because it is half in air and half in water.

Are stars star shaped?

No, stars are round like balls. We give them pointed edges when we draw them because this is what they look like from Earth, with their light blinking and twinkling.

What is a red giant?

All stars are born, live for a very long time, and then die. A red giant is a huge, ancient star.

Stars are being born all the time. They start their lives in star nurseries called nebulae.

1. All stars are born in huge spinning clouds of gas and dust. Our Sun was born 4.6 billion years ago.

3. Most stars are like our Sun and shine steadily for almost all their lives.

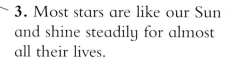

2. The gas and dust come together to make lots of balls, which become star clusters.

If you think of our Sun as shining like a car's headlights, then a red giant would shine like a lighthouse!

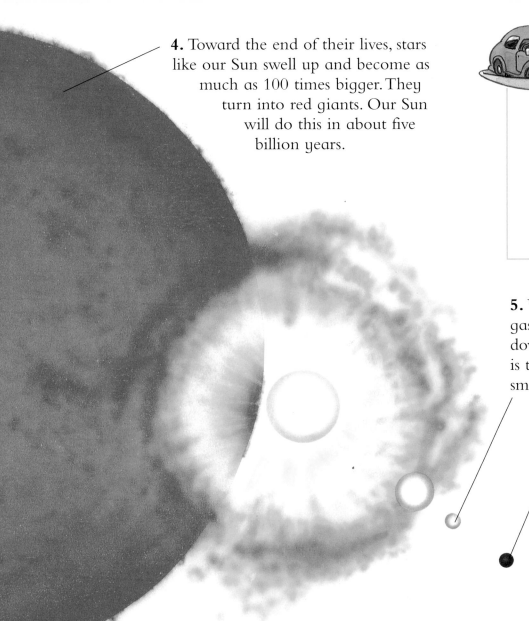

4. Toward the end of their lives, stars like our Sun swell up and become as much as 100 times bigger. They turn into red giants. Our Sun will do this in about five billion years.

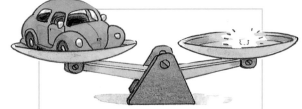

On Earth, a sugar-cube-size piece of a white dwarf would weigh as much as a small car!

5. When it has used up all its gas fuel, a red giant shrinks down into a white dwarf. It is then about 10,000 times smaller but still very hot.

6. The star cools down and ends its life billions of years later as a black dwarf—a cold, black cinder.

Stars must have at least eight times as much gas fuel as our Sun to end their lives in supernova explosions.

Which stars explode?

Different kinds of stars lead different lives. Some stars have a lot more gas fuel in them than others. These really massive stars do not die quietly by cooling down. Instead, they blow up in a huge flash of light. Stars that explode like this are called supernovae.

What is a black hole?

A black hole can happen when a massive star dies. The star falls in on itself, squashing all its material and becoming smaller and smaller. In the end, all that is left is a place from which light cannot escape—a black hole. Everything in space has a pulling force called gravity—galaxies, stars, planets like Earth, and even moons. Gravity holds things together and stops them from floating away into space . . .

Earth's gravity keeps your feet on the ground. It pulls you down and stops you from floating away into space.

When two large space bodies (such as a planet and a moon) get close enough, there is a pulling competition between their forces of gravity. It is like a giant tug of war.

. . . But stars that become black holes have very strong gravity—that is what pulls them inward and makes them collapse.

A planet's gravity holds its moons close to it and stops them from shooting off into space.

Light is sucked into black holes in much the same way as water is sucked down a drain.

A star that gets too close to a black hole is sucked into it. Nothing, not even the star's light, can escape the pull of the black hole's gravity.

How hot is the Sun?

Like all stars, our Sun is a huge ball of superhot gas. It is hottest in the middle—the temperature there is around 27 million °F (15 million °C). The outside of the Sun is a lot cooler than the middle—only 10,000°F (5,500°C). But this is still much, much hotter than the hottest oven!

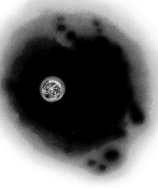

Most sunspots are larger than Earth.

Dark patches called sunspots come and go on the face of the Sun. They make it look as if it has the chickenpox. Sunspots are dark because they are cooler and so give off less light than the rest of the Sun.

Plants and animals could not live without the Sun's heat and light.

The Sun is the only star that is close enough to Earth for us to feel its heat. The next closest star to Earth is called Proxima Centauri. Our Sun's light takes 8.3 minutes to reach us, but Proxima Centauri's takes 4.3 years!

The Sun uses more than 30 million truckloads of fuel every second!

Will the Sun ever go·out?

One day, the Sun will use up all its gas fuel and die. But this will not happen in your lifetime, or your children's, or even your great-great-great grandchildren's! Astronomers think that the Sun has enough gas fuel to last for at least another five billion years.

20219145

How many planets are there?

Our planet, Earth, has seven neighbors. Together, they make up a family of eight main planets that travel around the Sun. We call the Sun, and all the space bodies that whirl around it, the solar system. Besides the Sun and the planets, the solar system includes moons, dwarf planets, asteroids, and comets.

Comets are rather like huge dirty snowballs. Most stay on the edge of the solar system, but a few travel close to the Sun. These comets grow gas and dust tails millions of miles long when the Sun's heat starts to melt them.

The word *planet* comes from the Greek word *planetes*, which means "wanderer."

Mercury Venus Earth Mars Jupiter

16

Sun

planet

orbit

An orbit is the path of a planet around the Sun, or a moon around a planet. The planets all have different orbits. Mercury is the closest planet to the Sun.

Millions of asteroids orbit the Sun in a belt between Mars and Jupiter. Some are like grains of sand. Others are as big as houses. A few are the size of Pennsylvania!

What is the difference between planets and stars?

Planets are not as big or as hot as stars, and they cannot make their own light. They were made from the leftovers of the same gas and dust cloud that gave birth to our star, the Sun.

Saturn

Uranus

Neptune

Why is Earth so special?

Our planet is the only one in the solar system with flowing liquid water and living things on it. That makes it very special. It is the third planet from the Sun, and it gets just the right amount of heat and light to keep us alive. Any closer, and it would be too hot. Any farther away, and it would be too cold.

When the Sun turns into a red giant star, it will swallow up Mercury and get so large that it will cover half of our midday sky.

All planets spin as they orbit the Sun.

You can see what happens as Earth spins if you turn a globe in the beam of light from a flashlight.

Why does the Sun go out at night?

It gets dark at night because Earth is spinning as it orbits the Sun. As parts of Earth spin away from the Sun, they move out of its light and into darkness. It takes a whole day and night for Earth to spin around once.

Astronomers think that millions of stars in the universe have families of planets. They have discovered more than 70 solar systems and are finding more all the time.

Which is the hottest planet?

Venus is not the closest planet to the Sun, but it is the hottest. The temperature there can reach 870°F (465°C). For comparison, the highest temperature ever recorded on Earth was 136°F (58°C), in Al'Aziziyah in the Libyan Desert, North Africa.

Although Mercury (right) is closer to the Sun, Venus is hotter! This is because Venus is covered by thick clouds of gas that act like a blanket, trapping the Sun's heat.

Space probes have landed on Venus and sent back pictures and information to Earth. The probes were destroyed soon after landing, however, by the superhot climate on Venus.

Mars is the next planet from the Sun after ours, and people once thought that, like Earth, it might have living things. Many space probes have visited, but they have not found any signs of life yet!

Which is the red planet?

Mercury is covered in craters—hollows made by huge space rocks crashing into it.

If you could visit Mercury, you would see that the Sun looks more than twice as big there as it does from Earth. This is because Mercury is so much closer to the Sun.

Mars is often called the red planet. The ground there is covered in dusty red soil that gets swept up by the wind to make pink clouds! The rocks on Mars have a lot of iron in them, and iron turns red when it rusts. A better name for Mars might be the rusty planet!

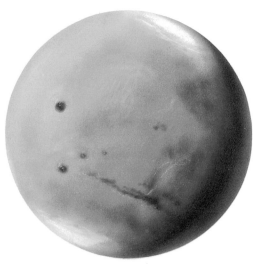

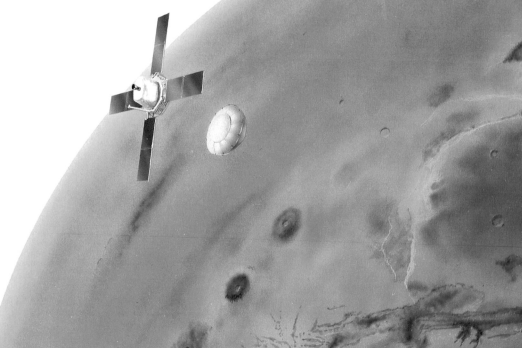

Living things need water. If there is any on Mars, it is frozen inside the planet's north and south polar icecaps.

Which is the biggest planet?

Jupiter is so huge that all the other planets could fit inside it! The beautiful patterns on its face are made by swirling clouds of gas, stirred up by powerful windstorms.

Jupiter's Great Red Spot is so big that two Earths could fit inside it! It is a gigantic storm that has been raging for more than 300 years.

Planet Jupiter was named by the ancient Romans after the king of their gods.

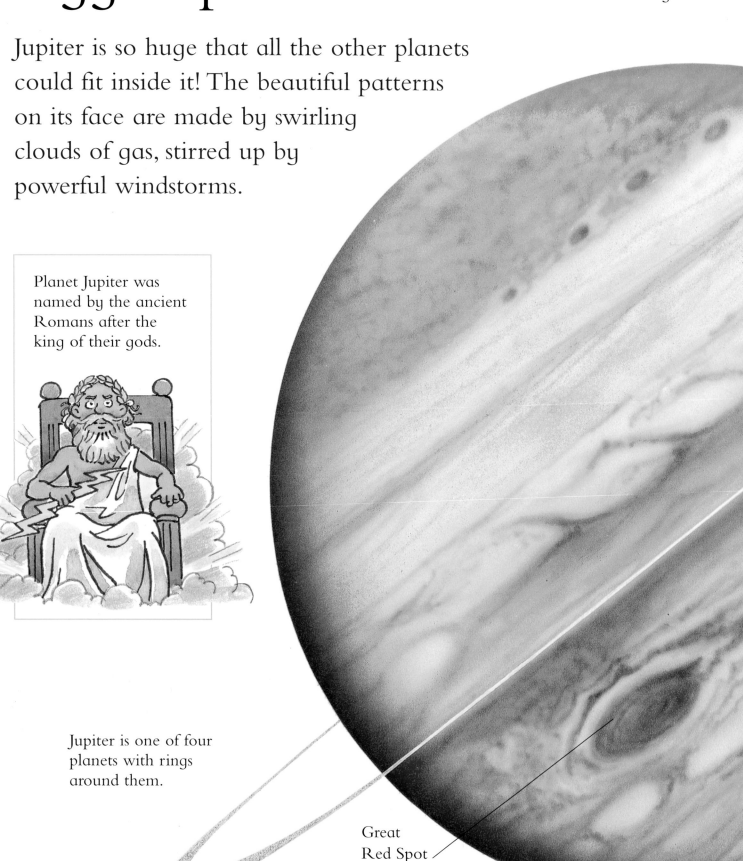

Jupiter is one of four planets with rings around them.

Great Red Spot

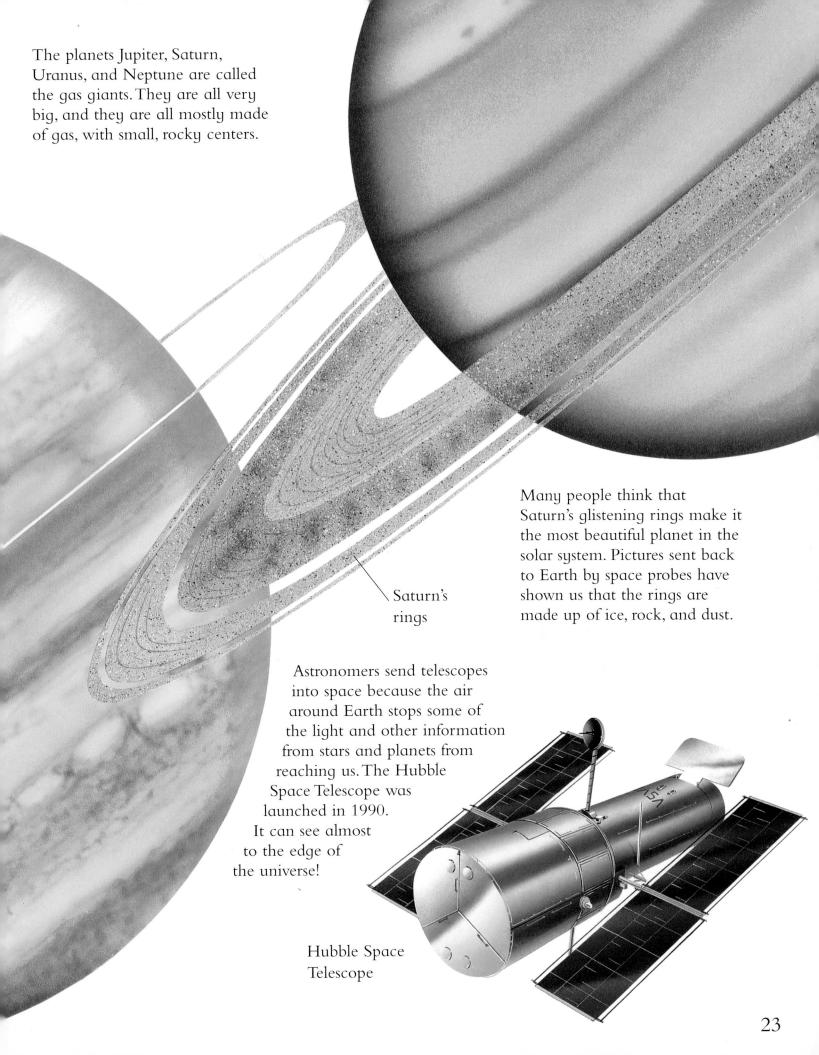

The planets Jupiter, Saturn, Uranus, and Neptune are called the gas giants. They are all very big, and they are all mostly made of gas, with small, rocky centers.

Saturn's rings

Many people think that Saturn's glistening rings make it the most beautiful planet in the solar system. Pictures sent back to Earth by space probes have shown us that the rings are made up of ice, rock, and dust.

Astronomers send telescopes into space because the air around Earth stops some of the light and other information from stars and planets from reaching us. The Hubble Space Telescope was launched in 1990. It can see almost to the edge of the universe!

Hubble Space Telescope

Which planet is the farthest from the Sun?

Neptune is the most distant and the coldest main planet. But beyond Neptune are at least 1,000 icy rock bodies called Kuiper Belt Objects, as well as the dwarf planet Pluto.

On Neptune, the temperature is an incredibly icy −330°F (−200°C). Even ice cream would taste as hot as soup on this planet.

Pluto was discovered in 1930 and was named after the Roman god of the underworld. It is now known as one of the solar system's dwarf planets.

Which planet is tipped over?

Uranus is the sideways planet. Its moons and rings go around its middle—but because it is on its side, they look as if they circle it from top to toe. Uranus was not always like this. It got knocked over by a huge asteroid when it was young.

How do we know about the farthest planets?

Until the American *Voyager 2* spacecraft visited Uranus in 1986 and Neptune in 1989, not a lot was known about these planets. *Voyager 2* gave us our first close-up look at these two distant worlds. The spacecraft's cameras showed us 16 of Uranus's moons and eight of Neptune's. Since then, more have been discovered using Earth's most powerful telescopes. Now we know that Neptune has 13 moons and Uranus has 27.

Voyager 2 left Earth in 1977 and reached Neptune 12 years later, in 1989.

Which planet has the biggest moons?

Moons are rocky bodies that orbit (circle) planets. Jupiter has at least 60 moons, and three of them—Ganymede, Callisto, and Io—are larger than Earth's moon. Mercury and Venus are the only planets that do not have moons. All the other planets have at least one.

Ganymede

Io

Callisto

Our Moon

In pictures taken by the space probe *Voyager 2*, Io looks like a giant cheese pizza. The red color comes from volcanoes.

What is it like on our Moon?

Earth's Moon is dry, dusty, and lifeless. There is no air to breathe or water to drink. During the day, it is so hot that your blood would boil. At night, it is freezing cold—not a nice place to take a vacation!

Which planet's moons look like potatoes?

Mars has two tiny moons that look like lumpy old potatoes. They are called Deimos and Phobos, and unlike larger moons, they are not round.

On July 20, 1969, two American astronauts became the first living beings ever to set foot on the Moon. Their names were Neil Armstrong and Buzz Aldrin, and their space mission was called *Apollo 11*.

If Earth were the size of an orange, then the Moon would be the size of a cherry.

The Moon's gravity is weaker than Earth's. You would be much lighter on the Moon—only one-sixth of your Earth weight. So you would be able to jump six times as high!

How fast can space rockets go?

Rockets have to travel faster than 7 miles (11km) per second to get into space. This works out to about 25,000 miles per hour (40,000km/h)—and car drivers can get into trouble for speeding at 70 miles per hour (110km/h)! If rockets did not travel so fast, they would not be able to escape the enormously strong pull of Earth's gravity.

Saturn V

The tallest rocket ever launched was Saturn V, which took the *Apollo 11* spacecraft into space and the first people to the Moon. It was more than 330 feet (100m) tall.

Ariane 4

space shuttle

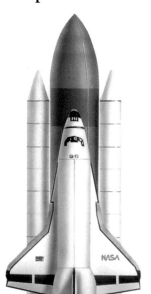

Rockets are made up of two or three parts called stages. Each stage is a giant fuel tank and engine that separates and falls away as soon as its fuel is used up.

At the top of a rocket is its payload—a satellite, a robotic space probe, or a spacecraft carrying astronauts.

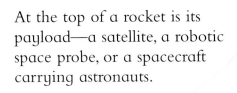

Satellites can be used by one country to spy on another country.

What are rockets used for?

Rockets are mostly used to put machines called satellites into orbit around Earth. Different kinds of satellites are launched to do many different jobs.

Satellite photographs and maps help scientists study Earth and what it is made of.

Communications satellites pick up and send TV and telephone signals.

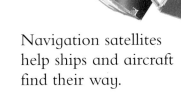

Navigation satellites help ships and aircraft find their way.

Some satellites help us figure out what the weather will be like.

Why do astronauts wear space suits?

There is no air to breathe in space, and depending on whether a spacecraft is in or out of the Sun's light, it's either very hot or very cold. Without space suits to protect them outside their spacecraft, astronauts would die.

Astronauts sleep in bags that are strapped down to stop them from floating. They even have to tuck or tie in their arms to stop them from waving around!

Astronauts have to wear seat belts to stop them from floating away when they use the toilet. Space toilets do not flush. Everything is sucked away instead.

Space stretches you—astronauts can come back to Earth as much as 2 inches (5cm) taller!

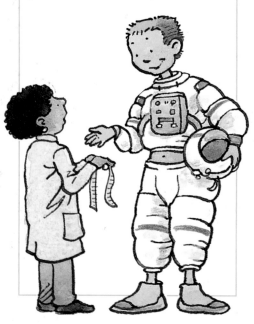

Why do astronauts float in space?

Gravity is everywhere. But astronauts on a spacecraft orbiting Earth do not experience it in the same way. The craft and astronauts are farther away from the pull of Earth's gravity, so they are actually "falling around" Earth rather than down toward it.

The gold visors on their helmets protect the astronauts' eyes from the Sun's harmful rays.

When they go on "space walks" outside a spacecraft or space station, astronauts work in pairs. One may be safely harnessed to a robotic arm (above), while another works nearby. On their backs they wear a life-support unit. This provides oxygen for the astronauts to breathe and pumps cooled liquid around their space suits to keep them at the right temperature.

Index

TITLES IN THE **I WONDER WHY** SERIES

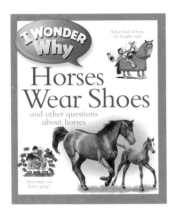

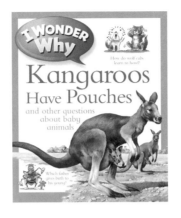

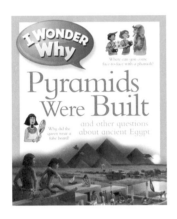

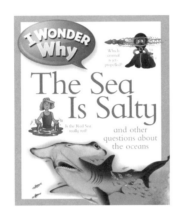

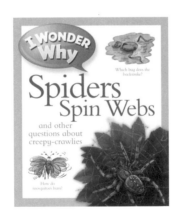

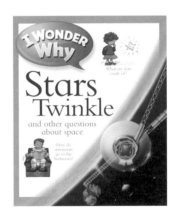

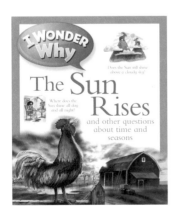

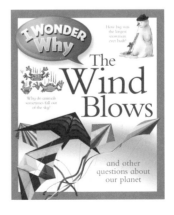